Every Man Is Innocent Until Proven Broke

Johnny Hart and Brant Parker

CORONET BOOKS
Hodder Fawcett, London

———————————————————

Printed and bound in Great Britain for
Hodder Fawcett Ltd, Mill Road,
Dunton Green, Sevenoaks, Kent by
Hunt Barnard Printing Ltd.,
Aylesbury, Bucks.

ISBN 0 340 21841 X

HOW COME WE NEVER TALK ANYMORE?

OTHER HUSBANDS TALK TO THEIR WIVES!...

YOU HAVEN'T SAID TWO WORDS TO ME ALL WEEK!

SHUT UP!

3·22

4-13

4.14

4-16

YOU HAVEN'T LOST
A POUND... YOU MUST
LEARN TO SAY NO.

HAVEN'T YOU
FINISHED YET?

NO.

CHOMP
CHOMP
CHOMP
MUNCH

4-23

WOULD YOU MIND TAKING OUT THE GARBAGE?

4.21

YOU EXPECT ME, THE MOST RESPECTED MAN IN THE CASTLE, TO LUG GARBAGE?

EITHER GET RID OF THE GARBAGE, OR I'M LEAVING!

THAT'S NOT MUCH OF A CHOICE.

3

5·1

5-3

5-4

5.14

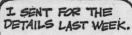

5-20

4

5-26

SQUEAK
SQUEAK
SQUEAK
SQUEAK
SQUEAK

IS MY WARRANTY GOOD FOR SQUEAKS?

FOLD
FOLD
FOLD
FOLD

IT'S WORTH A TRY.

6-4

5

SLURRP

6-28

PTOOEY!

THIS SLOP ISN'T FIT FOR MAN OR BEAST!

A SURPRISE FROM THE CHEF!

THERE'S **SMOG** OVER MY ENTIRE KINGDOM, WIZARD! GET **RID** OF IT!

BUT THAT'S **PROGRESS**, SIRE,.... MILLS, DUMPS, FOUNDRIES, TRANSPORTATION ....IT'S ALL MONEY IN THE ROYAL TILL!

.. EVER NOTICE HOW **PEACEFUL** IT IS, LOOKING DOWN ON A LOVELY, SOFT BLANKET OF SMOG?

7-9

7-12

7-15

7-16

FRIAR TUCK:
TO SEE YOU,
SIRE!

7:17

WHAT'S
UP
FATHER?

YOU KNOW, ... I'VE
BEEN WITH YOU SO
LONG, I'VE **FORGOTTEN.**

6

7-24

LEGEND HAS IT, THAT IF YOU KISS THIS ROCK, A HANDSOME, YOUNG PRINCE APPEARS.

SMACK

POOF

7-30

WE'RE GETTING CLOSE... IT'S HIS HORSE!

8-16

WHY DON'T YOU GET RID OF THAT THING?... HE GIVES ME THE CREEPS!

I WILL, AS SOON AS I FIND HIM A MATE.

A MATE?... WHERE IN THE WORLD WOULD YOU FIND ANYONE WHO....

8-20

CLOMP CLOMP CLOMP....

8-28

MY CLIENT DEMANDS TO KNOW THE CHARGE!

FIFTY DOLLARS OR FIFTY DAYS!

OBVIOUSLY, YOU ARE NOT FAMILIAR WITH JURISPRUDENCE....

9-3

FIFTY BUCKS FOR HER, TOO!

8

9-18

IT'S A BEAUTIFUL DAY... I'M GOING TO THE BEACH.

9·21

...BREW ME UP SOMETHING, SO I WON'T GET SUNBURNED.

MY HUSBAND, THE COMEDIAN.

THE BEST IN HUMOUR FROM CORONET

JOHNNY HART & BRANT PARKER

☐	21784 7	Life Is a 50p Paperback	50p
☐	21817 7	Frammin at the Jim-Jam, Fripping in the Krotz!	50p
☐	16476 X	The Peasants are Revolting	50p
☐	16899 4	Remember The Golden Rule	50p
☐	15818 2	The Wondrous Wizard of ID	50p
☐	18604 6	There's a Fly In My Swill	50p
☐	20776 0	Wizard of ID Yield	45p
☐	20529 6	Long Live The King	50p

All these books are available at your local bookshop or newsagent, or can be ordered direct from the publisher. Just tick the titles you want and fill in the form below.

Prices and availability subject to change without notice.

CORONET BOOKS, P.O. Box 11, Falmouth, Cornwall.

Please send cheque or postal order, and allow the following for postage and packing:

U.K. – One book 19p plus 9p per copy for each additional book ordered, up to a maximum of 73p.

B.F.P.O. and EIRE – 19p for the first book plus 9p per copy for the next 6 books, thereafter 3p per book.

OTHER OVERSEAS CUSTOMERS – 20p for the first book and 10p per copy for each additional book.

Name ....

Address ....

....